The Art of the Lonely Wanderer

Poems

Gbanabom Hallowell

Sierra Leonean Writers Series

Gbanabom Hallowell

The Art of the Lonely Wanderer
Copyright © 2016 by Gbanabom Hallowell
All rights reserved.

ISBN: 978-99910-54-31-5

Sierra Leonean Writers Series

The Art of the Lonely Wanderer

CONTENTS

Foreword by Dr. Ernest Cole	vii
Look At All the Lonely People	1
We Leave the House of Hunger	3
I'm Thinking About Taking a French Leave	5
I Left the Dark, the Unconscious	7
A Man Has Left Himself Behind	9
There Was a Twig Here Where I Stand	11
I Will Leave After Sex	13
Cain and the Second Migration	15
What About Those Who Left Yesterday	17
I Hear the Langoliers Are Coming	19
I Can No Longer Love You Here	21
My Head is Running Away From Me	24
The Journey Has Only Just Begun	26
Farewell to Everything Not Coming With Me	28
In Conversation with the Road	30
The House of No Return	32
Sailing On the Wings of Smoke	34
Of Sex, Exile and Longing	36
The River Runs Beside My House	38
I See Death Leaving By the Back Door	40
The Hour is About to Come	42
Rolling Stones	44
A Man is Moving Around in My Head	46
Liberty Left with a Pair of Slaves	48
My Wings Are Meant to Fly	50
A Solitary Bird Flies the Sky	52
When the Vulture Takes its Flight	54
I Got My Things and Left	56
After the Universal Romeo Had Died	58
Where Does Eternity Go From Here?	61
When the Soldier Goes to War	63

Of Hunters and Gatherers	65
A Rough Pair of Shoes on the Sidewalk	67
Have You Lost Your Mind?	69
The Naked Woman Goes in the Nude	71
Approaching Death from Another Man's Eyes	73
The Future of Stone	75
A Prayer For the Global Wanderer	77
Meet Me Wherever You Find Me	79
The Art of the Lonely Wanderer	81
Afterword by Dr. Lansana Gberie	85

The Art of the Lonely Wanderer

Other Books by Gbanabom Hallowell

POEMS

Hills of Temper (1996)
Drumbeats of War (2004)
My Immigrant Blood (2006)
Manscape in the Sierra: New & Collected Poems 1991-2011(2012)
A Little After Dawn (2013)
When Sierra Leone Was a Woman (2014)
Don't Call Me Elvis and Other Poems (SLWS, 2016)

EDITED BOOKS

Leoneanthology:
Contemporary Short Stories & Poems from Sierra Leone (SLWS, 2012)
In the Belly of the Lion:
An Anthology of New Sierra Leonean Short Stories (SLWS, 2015)

FICTION

Gbomgbosoro: Two Short Stories (SLWS, 2012)
The Road to Kaibara (SLWS, 2016)

WAR DIARY

Tears of the Sweet Peninsula:
May 25, 1997 and the Sierra Leone Civil Conflict (2005)

The Art of the Lonely Wanderer

"I got my things and left. The sun was coming up. I couldn't think where to go. I wandered towards the beer-hall but stopped at the bottle-store where I bought a beer. There were people scattered along the store's wide verandah, drinking. I sat beneath the tall msasa tree whose branches scrape the corrugated iron roofs. I was trying not to think about where I was going. I didn't feel bitter. I was glad things had happened the way they had; I couldn't have stayed on in that House of Hunger where every morsel of sanity was snatched from you the way some kinds of bird snatch food from the very mouths of babes."

Dambudzo Marechera, *The House of Hunger*

he who wanted to go far away, always farther away,
didn't know what to do there, whether he wanted
or didn't want to leave or remain on the island,
the hesitant one, the hybrid, entangled in himself,
had no place here

"The Weary One" Pablo Neruda

> Surely no one is with me,
> I don't mind, I don't need anyone;
> surely they have told me to go;
> I feel it clearly.

"The Accent Dangles" Cesar Vallejo

Gbanabom Hallowell

*This work is dedicated
to members of the Salone Writers Forum,
a Whatsapp group where we support
each other's effort to succeed as a writer*

The Art of the Lonely Wanderer

Gbanabom Hallowell

Foreword

In the Fall of 1995, I was invited by a group of Sierra Leonean poets to make a presentation at the USIS building at the American Embassy in Freetown. The presentation was based on my explication of the then recently published anthology *Lice in the Lion's Mane: Poets and Poems of Sierra Leone* (1995) by eminent budding poets. By then, I was Assistant Lecturer at my alma mater, Fourah Bay College, University of Sierra Leone. Gbanabom Hallowell's poems featured prominently in the anthology and they were among those I selected for critical analysis. A year later, he published his first collection of poems, *Hills of Temper* (1996), and I was again asked to present a review of the poems at the same location in Freetown. Both presentations met with huge acclaim and Gbanabom Hallowell and other budding poets were clearly identified as the emerging poetic voices of the future. Some eight years later, while in the United States, I learned that Hallowell had published another collection, *Drumbeats of War* (2004).

I make reference to the poet's work not only to acquaint readers with his writing or to merely characterize him as a prolific writer, but also to establish my familiarity with his poetic style and thematic preoccupations as social commentator, visionary, and teacher. This acquaintance allows me a literary space to construct a trajectory of his growth and development, frame his oeuvre as poet, describe the process through which his poetic concerns have come to maturation, and establish a set of critical formations as benchmarks to assess and interpret his works.

As I write the foreword to his latest collection, *The Art of the Lonely Wanderer*, a couple of things regarding the poet's style become evident in my mind. There is still the anger of the early poems, but this, in many ways, is now channeled into a more prescriptive and productive form of engagement with post-conflict Sierra Leone and the complications of peace after a decade of senseless carnage. As such, even though the poet draws from and inverts, if not subverts, biblical images, allusions, tropes and prototypes in exploring his rage and resentment at the state of his

The Art of the Lonely Wanderer

country, a style that recalls the poetic fervor of his countryman Syl Cheney-Coker, he does so "not as in the days of thoughtless youth," but as William Wordsworth in "Tintern Abbey" tells us "to recall the still sad music of humanity." In this conception of the poet's style, the music still stirs the soul but it also calms the emotions associated with the uncertainties and anxieties of the future. I suggest that even though the tidal waves are still beating wildly against the shores, the hills of temper have subsided and have been reconfigured and re-contextualized into social and political possibilities, while the poet has been, in Wordsworthian language, "chastened and subdued."

The Art of the Lonely Wanderer also registers a significant departure from the early poems, especially the linguistic difficulty and interpretive resistance with which the poet has been associated. Writing almost in the manner of Christopher Okigbo, or Wole Soyinka whom he admires, the early poems are characterized by dense symbolism, concentrated thought expressed in condensed language, obscure imagery and diction, and abstract ideological and philosophical references. The present collection, while still showing signs of thematic and stylistic continuities with the early poems, depict poems that demonstrate a more mature, analytical, deeply reflective, thoughtful, and logical writer. Hallowell has come of age, thematically and stylistically; his present collection reflects an acute mind that is aware that poetry is an interpretive activity and that meaning is layered, characters are complex, themes are nuanced, and style is complicated art. His collection has replaced sarcasm with wit, anger with logic, and breath of panorama with intensity of the gaze.

Hallowell's thematic preoccupations in the current collection also warrant critical commentary. The poems depict the writer's engagement with post-conflict Sierra Leone and his attempts at unpacking the complications of peace. While he draws from the causes of the civil war, he uses them as backdrop or canvas within which he paints the new Sierra Leone, one that is dealing with the legacies of the civil war.

Prominent in the collection is the journey motif, the desire, if not obsession with leaving one's homeland in search of a more stabled and prosperous, society. Working with this trope, Hallowell explores the interconnections between geographical space and individual and national identity within the conflicting and paradoxical contexts of staying and leaving, and memory and forgetting. A traumatic society confronting the legacies of its past, the journey is metaphorically one of self-discovery, of retracing the lost pathways, restoring lost values, addressing the causes of the societal malaise, engaging the social uncertainties and political anxieties of the present, and reclaiming the soul of the nation. The excerpts from Dambudzo Marechera, Pablo Neruda, and Cesar Vallejo provide a context for engaging the tensions between stasis and process, and to reconfigure the spatial binaries of inside and outside, margins and center, as well as restructuring the boundaries of self and other, inclusivity and exclusion, and of inequalities, and human suffering.

In this regard, images of the House of Hunger, the social and economic disparities, the burden of the past, the oppression of the present, and the uncertainties of the future serve as metaphorical constructs of social disempowerment and marginalization of the masses. Biblical prototypes of Cain, and historical figures as Hitler serve to establish the magnitude and depth of suffering in post-war Sierra Leone, while images of light and darkness, Eden and the fall of man, the desert and the storm, the vulture, rolling stone, tidal waves of the sea, and the violence of the ocean constitute physical and psychological trauma on both an individual and on a collective basis. Post-war Sierra Leone is a manifestation of the fruits of Eden, the consequences of disobedience and of the curse. The situation reinforces the curse associated with the mark and burden of Cain with its symbolic significance of violence, bloodshed, and death; in essence, a reversal of God's plan and purpose for humanity. Like Cain, Sierra Leoneans have become anti-human, what the poet refers to as the "humanimal," the "after-man," and the wanderer who has shirked his responsibility as his "brother's keeper."

In this circumstance, the human bonds of the beloved community have been ruptured and the poet sees it as his responsibility to call attention to the dysfunctional society and to engage in a search for the truth. The truth of post-war existence resides in the dilemma and complications of migration; a phenomenon to which the poet is at once ambiguous and ambivalent. While there is the tendency to flee, the state of the Diaspora and the nature and consequences of the journey speak a different truth. There is conflation of the Diaspora with the homeland and in this way the poet suggests continuities with the past. In both contexts, the destination of the traveler is elusive, the journey is fraught with dangers, and the consequences are loneliness, alienation, and death.

In spite of its challenges in dealing with the legacies of the civil war, the collection is strangely optimistic in depicting hope in post-conflict Sierra Leone. While he points out the disorientation in the present, Hallowell also emphasizes the possibilities. I suggest that even though the traveler is confronted with a dilemma he never fully comprehends and from which he never seems to be able to extricate himself, solace can be drawn from the awareness that the journey has only just begun. In the circumstance, hope resides in the fact that at least there is a road to traverse, and with resilience, fortitude, and faith, the future can be clearly shaped and distinctly mapped along lines of restoration and reconstruction.

Ernest Cole, Ph.D,
Associate Professor of English,
Hope College, Michigan, USA,
Author of *Theorizing the Disfigured Body: Mutilation, Amputation, and Disability Culture in Post-Conflict Sierra Leone*

The Art of the Lonely Wanderer

LOOK AT ALL THE LONELY PEOPLE

They come and go in large crowds, individually;
In infectious sorrow, and in the sorrow of their sadness.
A stick too is walking beside them, their aged lore,
Word of the old….. youth.
The stick besides
The aged walks like a staff in the crowd of lonely people.
The young, on their visible disorder, come on one leg
And leave on the other.
Proletarian, the lone wanderer
On a leg and a stick; the crowd
Walks his path with a mantle;
The city burns ahead of the crowd for want of fire!
And the lonely brothers drag their hurriedness along them
To reach the urban edge thirsting for life and burning down
To ashes for want of fire!

A deliberate crowd of lonely people,
Their sandals come in quick broadcasts…..
A breath over sound bites,
A dead man is walking his way to come back alive
In a crowd of lifeless people
Going home to home.
But the way the poet sees it, a piece of loneliness is too large
In the crowd, in the bottom and in the top, then it incarcerates
People….then where a bull of silence persists, the crowd,
Legendary in tradition, boosts its culture of crowdedness.
The people pick their steps from burden to burden,
With geographical disinterestedness; a gentle crowd
Is going up the hill and another is coming down.
Between them a child of pain occurs!

A crowd of one is coming against me, against my frontal
Being; then in all seriousness,
It is advancing as a crowd of twins,
Wearing the face of an old warrior.
In less than a minute the crowd
Swells to a hundred with a thousand
Sticks marching beside it.
The crowd is advancing, ceremonially.
The gold is ahead of it in its bullion, fleeing from the poor;
It is therefore not surprising to see that the numbered persons
Are fleeing the crowd, fleeing the sticks of crowd with a petroleum
Desire to catch up with the person in whom their lives are isolated;
That person not found in the crowd—even if the crowd
Is a billion miners, surgeons, a billion soldiers, a billion assistants,
Even if it's a billion one man, but not a single person!

WE LEAVE THE HOUSE OF HUNGER

We leave the house of hunger
For a place where food has been carted away;
Meeting with them that ate the leftovers of their own bellies.
In line with their philosophy, they join us to move the steps
Ahead of us in the rabid journey away from the fact
That was killing us below the beer served us in a mug
And tempered with loud calypso music.

That is all gone now like the blue sea always passing by one's door
With a mineral mind, and all one could do is to wave a hand
To the general storm. The waters of the sea have had their own
Arguments and so have we—we can now meet on the high edge,
Wave each other and pass by without an iceberg budging.

The house of hunger situates four cardinal ends, and
Could speak the revolution through
Its branches, and sing a song to its freedom from hunger.
It is precisely this moment that builds traffic in the dangerous
Sea-bed and we with our hunger, sing to the colorless flag,
That when our march is done we shall color the flag
The way we want it, and make it flag on our noses.

We are bending over backwards to move forward,
To march to where the general has planted a pole,
And where the profile is in readiness to define us as WE,
The group that became US in the history books with a single hair.
We shall reach the shore with an ambidextrous resolve:
To hold the flag in one hand and the color in another
And in that moment, a Blue Nile shall support our cause.

Gbanabom Hallowell

We have been told that away from the house of hunger
There is a big bowl of oatmeal, keeping warm, and when
We place the flag and the colors on the distant pole, we shall
Then settle to a common bowl.

Till then, Comrade, wear your veritable face and walk dutifully
On the palm fronds strewn your way. Approach your Jerusalem,
Fix an eye on the cup before it runs over,
And what content it shall spill
Ahead of you consider with every revolutionary bone in your body.
Pass beside the fallen heroes with biblical toes,
Remember them by name
Only when you stand before the altar; kiss your flag
Three times: two for the revolution
And one for the Comrade of the soil.
Remember you are a soldier of the house of hunger.
You left on foot where others have thought of flying; you braced
Your belly with a little anger to sweeten the journey on the sand.
Now that you have arrived, your journey has only just begun!

The Art of the Lonely Wanderer

I'M THINKING ABOUT TAKING A FRENCH LEAVE

I'm thinking about taking a French leave, about taking
A French leave, taking a French leave, a French leave,
French leave for a place similar to my current location:
A narrow door in the middle of a stone, and a dark stone
In the middle of a door. It means therefore, that I shall
Be leaving the work I do as a miner and offer my throat
To the pedestrian emptiness of the road.

I shall cast a tentative eye on the garrulous road
And take in the verdant absence
Of the celebrated scenery of the Garden of Eden
And then, in a rather obscene sense,
I shall narrow my gaze as if night
Is approaching me with a rough hand.

I shall wander to where there is an apostrophe on the soles of tired
Compatriots on the road and cast a deep thought on the value
We seek in the unknown world.
What is the breath of the green
Door we all seek to go through and who can say it will remain
Green through and through?

If I took a French leave, in respect of that,
I shall leave victims
Behind me. Each thing I get to leave with shall remind
Me of my betrayal. But who cares about the back
Of the back after one has turned one's face
Forward, looking at the mirage rattling ahead?
So that in taking a French leave, I shall put on the face of the new,
Forget about the usual blood that oozes from my miner's mouth.
I shall remember the daily dark pit I dug into, in which all I ever did
Was to create a black hole each hour.

I shall remember my coming up the pit with a rumpled
Face and fingers of gold, the taste of fire in my breath
And the iron muscles that made me super human.
My miner's mind shall remember the burning whisky
I gulped as a slave, and the sea I built in my belly rising to my brain.

If I took a French leave, just musing, taking a French leave,
From the presence of the reach of that German dog,
Whipping my back with words; my poor
Mind is just wandering how a French leave,
I would take could bite
The balls of that German dog, sleeping in his Hitler bunker.
His black whore with her rabid eyes would like to know what
Took me off their grip? What temerity
I had to leave a house that would be divided between itself?
What sorrow the pits would have outside in the cold,
Not feeling my black hand on their open mouths,
To swallow me whole and humble me. The pits would no longer choke
of the alcohol in my small flask.

I'm thinking about taking a French leave,
About taking a French leave,
Taking a French leave, a French leave, French leave.
If I took a French leave in Africa, I shall walk to the Nile
In search of clean water, and then I shall turn
Toward the Sahara desert to search for a road to traverse.

I LEFT THE DARK, THE UNCONSCIOUS

I left the dark—the unconscious,
Unpacked, hooking unto someone's cord.
A flight of blood, not a red experience on my way.
A locomotion came alive and a train, derailed,
Since its own life also came alive. Someone shot a gun
Several months ago, not to kill any object, just a shot
For fun, and in the distance of a persistent shadow
It all turned serious—in that little breath of space,
Nothing prevailing, the shooter packed up his bag and left.

I came, leaving for someplace, maybe for no place.
Maybe for a while I left a corner of my mind
Walked to another, thinking between two corners,
Thinking about all the things there were to pack,
Leaving the bits in which they were made to live together;
But in the ancient matter of one leaving for some other place,
All I needed was to be pushed out of another's flesh.

Flesh *off* flesh, my journey took a position;
I cried because I was leaving to go, to go, and not to return;
In the journey I thought more about a return.
I didn't begin to think about when hunger and I laid
On the same bed in the affair of our point of no return.
That was the moment something beat within me, my heart.
I cried for love, the absence of which had sent me leaving.

It's funny how things you didn't pack show up in the bag, laid
Like it was done by a hand that must go somewhere; how it
Patiently waits along the line of other packed items;
How it remains silent until woken by the tired heart, the sore
Soles, touched by the wearied hand, and breathed on

By the lazy nose and then used like a traveling partner.

My hair wasn't there. It came in the dark, breaking
Through my unsuspecting skin with a fierce pinch; then came
My anger smelling as if from a thousand miles away,
Tearing my bag for a place to lie or temper down.
In that pandemonium, came my fear, sauntering into
The shy pockets of my bags, coming along with the mind
Of a snake, bruised on the head. Following after was my temper
Full of the smell of alcohol—when it came the room was hardly
Enough for all the unkempt others that had scurried here and there
Panting as if they had left the past long before now.

A MAN HAS LEFT HIMSELF BEHIND

A man has left himself behind looking for someone ahead of him
As he heads for a place people go to discover themselves; their
Bodies, leaving themselves behind. The man,
Behind, hangs over the packed bags for breath, for the energy
Spending itself within the mind of its own science.

The traveling man is two men in physics, brewed in the hasty
Laboratory of shallow hills, rugged mountains and bitter leaves
In fading forests, in warm water rushing into valleys high and low.
He lifts up his eyes and a house goes ahead of him,
Taking with it the things that cannot be packed in a bag.

This man is in search of Dambudzo Marechera, to accompany him
To where the journey is on-going, where the destiny is the edge
Of the world, liberating itself from other edges;
A pair, he hopes they both can sweat together in color
And in resolve, keeping in mind that
One must always get up and go.

The road is passing him by with a load of arguments on its neck.
Too many people had stepped on its ego—the burdens
Of the steps occupy the mind of the road, the terracotta mind
Of the long winding road the man who left
Himself behind walks on,
Swinging two anxious hands.

The body of the road is tense tonight, and the man is walking
On it undecidedly, walking on it because he is searching for a man
Called Dambudzo Marechera. Everywhere he goes
He is told that Dambudzo Marechera
Just left after getting his things;

Gbanabom Hallowell

He is told to go right, left, right again, and
To finally go around himself twice; maybe, just maybe,
Dambudzo will be busy walking into people with his Marechera.

People walk on the road having got
Their things; but here is the otherwise lonely road
With no things to pack, and people don't have
The decency to ask the road where it is going. They come
And leave, drunk and dirty.

Hey, all you people, a man is looking for Dambudzo Marechera
Along the road; but maybe he is not on this road but on another.
What matters is that a man is on the road searching, and if he is not
Able to see Dambudzo Marechera,
Maybe he can start searching for himself.
This man searching for Dambudzo Marechera left himself behind,
And it is doubtful whether he will ever see himself, even
Before he sees the man called Dambudzo Marechera.

The Art of the Lonely Wanderer

THERE WAS A TWIG HERE WHERE I STAND

There was a twig here where I stand
And then a happy leaf on it rattled green
In its own apex, celebrating a fed stomach;
Then the fig saw a big desert approaching,
Full of sand, terracotta sand, coming
With a ferocious heat.

The desert was a haunch with a belly full of hate;
The sun had pissed on it all day until it turned
A gold of anger with no oases to calm it down.
The extension became a journey;
With a bag full of anger, the desert puked
Elsewhere the gold that fattened its belly.

The leaf saw nothing coming, occupied
With its own full stomach, it kept shaking
In its green standpoint, shooting power
From the foundation of the twig,
Rattling all the more, full of the hunger
Of joy, the leaf rattled even greener.

O tropical leaf, fed in your photosynthesis,
You flailed in the wind in green suit but the brown
Came with the desert, sewn to fit,
To take away your youth while it was still day,
To waste your mind with a grain of sand
And to break your courage at a bend.

A lone twig, brown all over, a lone leaf,
Green like a child—the desert packed
Its brown bag and it left like a drunk, ruffled

By the wind passing by as always, to quench
An occasional thirst in the ocean, even in the Nile,
To quench the fire that threatened to make it visible.

There was a strange feeling between leaving and staying.
One poet, Cesar Vallejo, distant in time, called it a Nativity Relief.
But what about the distance of arrival where one left to go?
What about the moment the bucket spilled its water on the ground,
When every soil got wet in its complete entirety,
Couldn't it be said that a journey had fallen in trance?

Little birds made a noise for the single green leaf on the foundation
Of the brown twig, unaware that its end was nigh; for it would
No longer be a green leaf once the journey commenced.
The tidal waves dashed with a great force, sweeping
Gentle or violent trees. How sad that the beautiful
Green leaf, with its entire continental blade, vanished
Without packing!

I WILL LEAVE AFTER SEX

I will leave after sex for the century that just passed me by.
Behind me is a soul seeking life in grand style
And already too many days are falling off its resolve, and
Not to mention that too many red angels are befriending me.
I will leave after sex with a new name and like new breasts
I will bathe in the foam between the two centuries; and when
The threshold is in its forgetful state, I shall abandon
The soul already ravished by your sex and jump for the moon.

I set my foot on a stone and a long memory stands tall in my head
Breathing like a sea, looking to merge with the ocean,
An ocean itself forcing to fit between common slippers
Which knows the road where water never comes to an end.
Pardon my belching; sex always digs deep into my gut
For a golden coin that turns into brass when fished out
Of the ocean, an ocean that runs backward
In search of a century of water thirsting the years before it.

A man is masturbating on the road; I do not know which way
He intends to go with his appetite in his face
After his one man labor. But here I am subject of the end product
Of sex, stopping to judge or to observe another who only
Had sex under his armpit. Which way he will go, I do not know.
I do not know where I am going either, except that I am
Taking a centurion walk below my belt where my pants were down.

A sudden woman is on the bed of the century where water flows
Into oceans and her sexual looks are making my own progression
To the affairs of the past difficult.
What syllable shall I utter to scare her away?
To belittle her urge, whatever it may be? I am holding

An appetite in my hand, determined to go back in time where
I shall grow into a youth and launch a comeback into thoughts.

I am entering the colony of time where, no matter the strength
Of my philosophy, I shall forever be two in one person;
Linguistically speaking, I shall be the one who utters and the one
Who is uttered to; my attention has suddenly been brought
To the colonial rule about people who make love
And migrate to the center core of their psyche.

They shall not be held responsible for their own death if it happens
Where time has tangled with place, where men become perishable,
Running to catch up with their imaginary selves.
Therefore, if a blade is necessary at the end of every century,
There has to be a resolve to help out with what kind
Of people who bend backwards,
Who dare to believe they have always been two people living apart
In time and in distance.

The Art of the Lonely Wanderer

CAIN AND THE SECOND MIGRATION

The dutiful murderer
Was the first vagabond heading anyone's way, killing
With a rage he who must set fire from the sky.
After his envy had subsided, he got his things and left,
Leaving a father and a mother to commit suicide
In the Garden of Eden before they jumped into fire
giving birth to a humanimal below the garden's ego.

A legion of one, Cain waved goodbye to man and became
The after-man, and his sun gaped at his moon into
The journey that was never meant for a place or a stop.

Cain, the native dragon drew his last human breath
When crossing the sin porch of his mother. Apple son,
The mortal tooth took its bite on the soft human flesh
And it was Adam who raged in agony, having been
Hurt in the rib cage, his cat life was already in God's hands.

O God, Cain had no time for you. You didn't own a car
To run him down the bridge where Abel's dogs drank their thirsts
In his blood, neither did you own a Bible to push it down his lips.
A cloud stood between you and Cain and you wanted him
To be his brother's keeper?

In faith, the son was a red eye and his journey took the way
Leading to Jerusalem even if palm fronds
Were a fiction of the mind,
Not that Jesus mattered in this experimental humanity.
Judas was enough in this journey as long as he didn't stop
To save any crude oil. Everything would be saved for Hitler
Because Cain loved him so much.

Cain left his home in jeans with a holster and a gun,
A heart full of bullets; no place for a brother's keeper,
A thirst in a punch bag, a mantle full of pride, a rocket
Aimed at heaven, and a footnote to his animalistic being.

That night after killing Abel, Cain stole into the Garden of Eden
And climbed up the Tree of Good and Evil, carting away
The atomic bomb. On the way out he bruised the snake
On the head and gagged it to puke its tongue; there he beheld
The atomic code across the red flesh of Lucifer. A host of former
Angels were on the heels of Cain. He left the perimeter
Of the garden in an electric train, headed either West or South.

WHAT ABOUT THOSE WHO LEFT YESTERDAY

What about those who left yesterday
In the middle of the soft painting? What about
Their footprints at the edge
Of our palms? They left for Libya
So that they can leave by boats. The food left for the grinder,
Even in this house of hunger.

What about the loud silence left behind
By the mourners? The pain they imported
From Gethsemane and Jabesh Gilead?
What about the blue vultures
Who circled above us yesterday? Ancient afternoons
Ate insects to stop them from flying.
By night when sporadic colors came from burnt fires
Screaming logs found refuge in our eyes.

What about
The broken questions and the voodoo
Of their broken Nile? What bait was stringed on the line to solve
The problem of the poor who left
With those who left yesterday? Who benefited from the accurate
Truth of poetry when Wole Soyinka was
A priced commodity? The men have left with all their magic,
And all around us the only available knife left
Is going after ordinary men to cut their throats
For blood, cocktail blood, hot for desert anxiety.

Boralakoh is in the street crying for children above the average
Pendulum of death and in spite of their party in the eyes
Did someone mention in her cry something
About the blood of the Sierra? O Sierra, what cheek

Did Pedro kiss you on? That Portuguese sailor
Who packed up his bags and came?
Sierra, there is severity in your eyes.

Have you been
Weeping for your children who are leaving for Libya
To leave by boat? Sierra, half of you is not looking too well.
It is clear that your soul is feeling like a dead horse
Unleashed to find refuge around islands of dead water
Where music plays tired notes in beaten waves.
The place is now empty, cleared of the lazy things.
Of all the people who have left for Libya
Or for other places, like Nigeria or Seychelles
Two places that have learned to be far from each other,
A new republic is born in exile.

But the new people suddenly paused their drumming of the sea
And of the hearts they brought with them. No, they have not
Yet arrived where their music will echo itself.
Where they had arrived, they suspect
It was a place of departure, and the sonorous waters
Would never merge with their own beginning,
Even if it were in hard
Books or stone covers. The island is temporary in the heart
And it will begin to sink, to disappear,
Just like everything that must pack up and go!

I HEAR THE LANGOLIERS ARE COMING

I hear the Langoliers are coming?
They ate the building I had my things in.
With sharp edged anger, they consumed
The foundation profile.

Perfidy in the teeth, close touch
Of a smile as brown as body and no soul,
As body as earth, witnessing the end,
The final reunion.

Metal men, half-men, jaw size
Existence in upper cut, a form moving
Life in bits, in holding unto the efficient bit;
And eventually merging as a whole giant
With an appetite to hunger for the chase.

Who sees a Langolier sees death
Sitting on the seat of his happiness, and
Aiming to pick a cup in his blood.
Alas, this must be said in cold blooded truth.

We must keep our lives alive.
And the submission is that we must leave,
We must wrestle gently with the future
Now that it is soft before our faces.

The Langoliers are approaching, electrically.
Our throbbing heartbeats quicken their steps.
Don't sit lazily on your own curiosity.
Fear can gather us to an early death.

A tenth in hand is better than a whole in a trap.
Run with your moral energy.
Grab the wind by its conscience and flee;
Pursue yourself and you will be faster than light.

Conjure safety from the corner of your thought
And bring your body to the safety of the net.
I hear the electricity of the Langoliers
And the urgent and primal being of their nature.

Celestial being urgent on my person and my blood
What swift fire turns you against me and my kind?
Tonight I relocate both in body and mind
To make you conqueror of an empty space.

By my leaving, you fear the prominence of your empty victory,
The bloodless engagement of your violence turns you into a victim;
Abstract body, of being, unravel the science in your existence,
This victory could kill you if you should know too much.

I CAN NO LONGER LOVE YOU HERE

Back of the front of this house there is a mind that died
Last night, and whether the back door is removed and erected
On the left side of the structure, the house itself can no longer
Live longer than the life of a plucked rose. So, it is useless to talk
About dusty pictures as if their portraits will come to life; ignore
All the other dead belongings, walk out in silence and pluck
A life from the fig tree three meters away.

I do not think like a zombie or a vampire. I wrestle
With the principalities I have grown among: their lavender grey,
And all the others that scrape the lilacs
With the torment of an Ancient
Testimony of arts. Everything now lies before us, watching us kiss
With dead eyes, but the blue minds that gave us Cupid's hunger
No longer linger in the house; therefore, a decision shall
Have to be made, to judge all these dead who would
No longer be able to judge us.

How can I assure you that the golden dream left this abode
Immediately after our wedding, without putting your eyes
To eternal tears? The cold
Impartial lightening of the candles on the table
The night I hugged you
Stole a piece of ornament from between us.
So that even when we answered
In the affirmative to the love that came from
The rector's mouth I discovered
That no sound accompanied our words.
It is too late to invite the tired
Passion of the Church of God.
Men no longer walk on ladders of hope.

How can I make love to you on dead foliage
In an inside that walked out of itself to surrender
To the burning city in which the house lived?
In repose, our wedding; love is in madness
Over the silence of words.
The continental effort of this house to imprison
The remaining lives
Hanging to witness the end will not see a lamp to guide it.
Last evening, the remaining volumes of poems
Slid by the front door, taking
Along the flint that lit for us in the waiting room.

We must leave before love leaves us
And before our single body is divided
Into two; let us leave here naked
As if we are walking into the Garden of Eden.
Entrepreneurial lover, the habit of this house is to demolish itself
And to lie on the foot of its nothingness;
The dark man can no longer
Suspend his hammer; tonight it must come down like a plough.
Take my hand persistently and love me against your body.
In a few minutes when this house shall come against itself,
I want to be remembered as a man!

From this vegetable house we must make our flight.
Two odours are reconciling into one thread, one long Babel
Of thread, to pull us into its superficial grips.
Cast your eyes love, on the ruins
That no longer constitute a house.
The four walls have lost their twin sons;
Therefore, the house shall burn without a powder.
The fire consuming
The house shall pass by immemorially,

Burning only in its own pain;
And from a distance, you and I shall weep for joy.

MY HEAD IS RUNNING AWAY FROM ME

My head is running away from me.
O Man, stop me at the winding stream,
Let me drink from your two palms.
I will pause as long as I am the owner
Of my head. But today, it feels like my head is leaving me, and
Chatting its way by the general stream.
What instance has come upon my head?
Tie me to a tree to turn my blood to green.
Allow my legs to dig deep into the soil of my kith
For I cannot afford my head to leave me.
How can my mind rush into the middle of my head?

Look beyond your eyes, my head could be passing
You by on the street with its intended logic
As to why it wants its own freedom from me.
I am in the village square pointing
Which way to go chasing after my head,
After its panting face and widening nose,
After its ears, falling deaf on solid places.
It's all coming back to me, pressing against my body
Where philosophy could sink in if mankind never had a head.
It's all holding a golden candle to my blue belief,
That I am master of my head.

O head, why run to places you cannot later remember
Without me, and to places you can only reach by sticks,
Gazing at things you do not have a heart to conceal?
Do not go consuming all the hungers
Of the world without a place to store your own.
Return from the stone of your thoughts and embrace
The humanity you have left behind you.

The Art of the Lonely Wanderer

You are a person made of my parts,
There is nothing therefore you can do
To live apart from me who have carried you with ease.
Do not let your tongue taste the distance on its own.

I have a baptismal duty to keep you safe in this experimental world.
Implacable hands can ruin your six senses. Therefore, come to me
With a Sunday smile, approach me as if I am an altar; bow in regret
And reconcile with the body of man.
Your days shall be my days.
It is my echo that goes into your ears
To make you see the wisdom of blood.
Only together as one could we become the son of man.
Only then could the river
Hesitate to cart away our wet clothes on the rock beside it;
Only then could the rectitude of our single being be recognized.

Where goes my head at this uncomfortable hour
When green knives breathe the black air of the night?
Can someone illustrate the pain I feel at the top
When Monrovia sheds its tears from the neck
And Freetown goes about like a drunkard? O Conakry,
Go under your rainy season and touch the body
Of the oases to calm your restless veins.
Touch a stone where it is warm and lead yourself by the bleeding
Neck, dear Banjul. The unpardonable hour is becoming clearer
In its defiance of my plea, be ready to prepare a road
For the hanging head of Africa.

THE JOURNEY HAS ONLY JUST BEGUN

The Journey has only just begun. The immediate past
Has instantly become the far past. The road lies ahead
Into the mirage of a future history. The present is reclining
And all the water has poured itself to soften the terracotta
Brother, and the lingering sister who have both
Been consumed by wandering.

How sad, the water has become wet, soaked all over its suit.
And now it cannot change its dress in the middle of this important
Footsteps. Wet, even in mud, early in the journey it begins to limp.

A temper has just passed us by like lightening,
With a load on its head.
The road trembled beneath us in that instant, and a tooth fell
From the mouth of the wind. Who's there up in the sky
To help us have a smooth sail on this journey?

Ahead of us a small man has just hit his left toe against
A hidden rock and blood is oozing from the collision.
For that man the journey has almost come to an end.
He sits there with a grim face, waiting...
Who's there up in the sky to put a smile on his face?

A woman is pursuing herself in the middle of the road
Over the black bird that shaved the head of her husband.
Even early in the journey,
When fourteen steps have not been achieved,
Fourteen thoughts short of a theory, the journey is still around
The immediate periphery of a cold hard slab.
This afternoon the new journey will no longer be fresh; therefore,
Anguish is expected to join the team that is no longer sticky.

The Art of the Lonely Wanderer

But whoever brings a bandana will carry a handkerchief with him.

The journey has only just begun and already no one has left.
The establishment is folding its mat ready to set foot on the road.
Nothing else is suspending itself but the souls of the eager ones
Have stood ahead in conjuring the distance.
Who's up there in the sky
To tell how long the journey is going to last?

Dondodo has got his things to leave;
Minkailu got a handful of happiness
In his bag to leave; Mambu, the town crier got his microphone
To leave; Feremusu has distanced herself from the fire believing that
The journey feeds the hunger of the soul;
Ferenkeh has packed his jug
Of wine with a mind drunk for the journey.

What no one knows is that Tempest is embarking on this journey
So also is Gloom; but Calm is hanging on to the clergy's mind.
This morning, the journey, has only just begun.

FAREWELL TO EVERYTHING NOT COMING WITH ME

Farewell to everything not coming with me.
I say farewell to my soul which walked out of me in the rain
And glowed like a cemetery
To the cemetery not responding to my call
To the call not spewing with words
To the words not formed in sound
To the sound not touched by an organ
To the organ not breathing in its thick skin
To the skin not dead in its corpse
To the corpse not waking in its comfort
So farewell to everything not coming with me
To the bridal cathedral where I couldn't break a broken marriage
To the broken marriage beating upon my brow
To my brow drained of its bravery
To the bravery drenched in its soul
Farewell to my infant tooth that went
Away with its undiscovered childhood
To the tooth's undiscovered childhood spent without its logic
To the infant logic lost in philosophy
Farewell to the good harvest and to the bold
Fruits of domesticated trees
To the anthem of the harvesters that rang over the humble hills
To the barns that kept the secret of hunger
To the night watch against pilfering
To the neck of the woods where silence reigns supreme
To the utter silence of quietness
Farewell to the duty station that left its doors
Open to the night of the dark
To the general who checks on it even in his sleep
To the blue pen which took in the pains

Of birth and painted my face in class
To the same place that was the same place
To the stone that sat on the humble hill
To the wolf that came by every night to scavenge
To the spoons and gaping pots and pans that go to bed hungry
To the too much that came out too little
Farewell to the parish priest who broke bread with me man to man
To Pa Beareh, the ultimate poro man, who sang long dirges in tears
To the festival of the moon which joins in choruses
To the stone that has sat 1000 years near the stream
Without laughing from a tickle
To the river that runs as if it is rotating
To the pure of the night falling from the sky without weight
To the weight of the day
Dropping hard from the compound of the sun
To the pint that holds the alcohol for the sake of the stomach
To the stomach that holds the alcohol for the sake of the head
To the head that holds the alcohol for the sake of the brain
Therefore, farewell to the secretary of hope and the clerk of papers
To the bitumen that paved the road I shall forever travel
To the construction worker laid to rest beside his concrete anarchy
And to all that have passed through the eye of a needle, farewell…

Gbanabom Hallowell

IN CONVERSATION WITH THE ROAD

Man to Road

Laid, absolute of mind, extreme terracotta behavior,
You are in your lane, bringing to merge the past, present and future.
Throbbing heartbeat, your brown moves figuratively into thoughts,
Into the thick of green forests, audacious and red
In theory of clearly
Essential nature. You, in your persuadable narrative,
Nothing of the past,
Present or future is hidden from your length.
What pedestrian weight makes you groan in utter guttural sound?
And to say that ten days on
Your back has not even made you frightened me?

Road to Man

Of quick heels and swift tongue, you must approach the universe
By its expanse. Double up and reverberate your pulse. Your soles
Are warm, truly, servant of your mind.
Walk upon my breath judiciously,
Bruise my back; I feel the pangs of a slave. Step your being on my
Dustbowl, and I will begin and end
The journey with you ponderously.

Man to Road

Maybe you are philosophical,
Socialist of mind; all on board your brown
Academy. The gallops are listening to you.
They appear spontaneously under the leg,
Bruising the shoe at its apex of ego; between where you hum

The Art of the Lonely Wanderer

And the lugubrious steps of man,
An immense clockwork is engaged
To keep note of the interaction made
Through times change and locomotion.
Collecting accurate knowledge of persons plying you dutifully,
And the not so dutiful legs hastening in thought
Yet motionless in warmth.
What creature creeps in your belly poking fingers in your throat?

Tell me O Road, do you ever leave when I leave?
Once you feel my weight do you get your things and leave with me?
How so you wake up to go?
You keep me company with an enormous mind,
Where do you meet me
Momentarily to converse with me?
I flee on thee, how do you flee with me?
Maybe you contemplate the man
Who takes a step on you, who savours
Your grandeur in practical steps?
You wait methodically and listen to the rhythm
Of the goer who comes on your wait.

THE HOUSE OF NO RETURN

I wrapped my naked skin around my soft home
And together we left the house of no return.
The door was against me and against my return.
The window did not accept me in the midnight sun.
I left the house of no return, foiled in the leaves
Of my singular home. I went up the mountain of my hope
And I said to myself as if I spoke to another,
That the house below the ego of the mountain no longer
Opened its blatant door to anyone
Who has left; therefore, not to me.

Yesterday the house sought to reconcile with its bricks
And to seek after the titles of its firmness, to stand the ground
Where it planted its image; the solid favor of its building
Held against the corner breasts of its rejected stones,
Leaping above its extremity to announce a voice in its long
Patience, and in the body that never laid the foundation of a Corpse.
The pillars are huge and so are their armors; breastplates, with an
investment of steel, I bear you no grudge.

In the time my little hands stretched to take notes of their exile
The house had migrated three sides of its diary, and the little
Window that got constructed before the big door came with
Its little book, hooked unto its hinges. Now you stand as a landlord
Waiting only on your own self; beside your ownership, stands
The pail that painted you, that milked you with its two breasts;
And you kept the eight brushes that gave you your dignity,
Sweeping the smooth bricks on the silent gesture of your grace.

I have not yet turned my eyes against the edges of your story;
And that is not likely to happen

The Art of the Lonely Wanderer

Ten million miles away from your soul,
Because it is impossible to smell distance in you whether I leave
Or you sit upon yourself naked. In want of a three-quarter trust
I will miss the centuries in your broad rooms and the periods
That roamed in them. The creatures of exile that came prodding,
Chasing the ultimate maid of your yellow fire, licking tremendous
Salt at dinner table, and eventually, collapsing in dark places,
In the sonorous house of no return.

Tonight, my time goes up in the house of no return;
A rude stick leads the way, and the journey
Hiccups on its own palm, belching a civilian honor
To the road, to the impala
Ahead, hastening to the undecided desert
With a resolve more social than mine.

SAILING ON THE WINGS OF SMOKE

After my broom had combed the sea with its wizardry
The expanse laid its sexual waters whorish blue temper.
It was its manual innocence that tempted my flight with speed.
A sweet smoke is on my heels, coming with platonic amber.

Then, beneath my industrial attempt at embracing
The sea, the smoke, now algebraic in motion, puffed a ribbon
Around my heart, majestic; And evolving from its dark energy,
Addictive of claim, it took control; Membrane, two clouds,
Oftentimes of one cloud, oftentimes divided.

Fierce smoke on water, the miles are shouting beneath the bed,
Beneath the teeth of the combed waves; the broom in its wizardry
Had tied the breath of the sea to its straws and sank its gaze with
Cologne; the sea is perishing at the tail of the smoke and I am
Casting my gaze ahead.

The centuries are passing me by in their bullets.
They are motionless in their speed, halted by my own advance,
They swiftly run by me without moving, without blinking
In their sonnets or in their careful
Verses, granted sound by the lyre of the smoke.

Two boys are panting on the left;
They have lost their energy to the wind.
A memory, dripping of blood is tumbling
Ahead, having lost its way in the fog.
A dog is barking at me, asking that its name be pronounced twice.
A bird is coming hard on to itself, seeking to defy its future corpse.

The Art of the Lonely Wanderer

Two answers are seeking after a question in the salubrious
Wind; a long awaited medical solution jumps excitedly
Over a new corpse; two stanzas are teaming up
To become one collaborating eye; at the torrential hour,
A door and a window are struggling to go into each other.

The smoke beneath me braces itself against
The agony of its own speed. I am clung to its base,
To its double persona, expressing my contradiction
Under the nascent clouds, the erstwhile desire
To transport a man from fire to fire in less than an aggressive
Speed, is coming now as a current of truth.

The journey is in full smoke and all the fires have been consumed,
The steel of the sky has melted into liquid, drinking its own pride.
The wind is burning in its element behind us,
Dying in the dead hours; any bridge left hanging after
We have passed lost an eye in the smoke.

Every so often my corpse surges in my body
As the speed of my flight goes to the corners where a sound collapses
For want of capacity. I have become a guest
In my own body waiting in the corner of my mind
For the evident man on this journey, left-handed in thought.

OF SEX, EXILE AND LONGING

Despair has come over the little man in the rain
Waiting to find his lips to say a little prayer.
His mind is more set on the woman last night
He couldn't bed than it is on God.
He contemplates sex in the form of a prayer and curses the woman
Under his stained breath. His mind takes a leap and clutches
The beer he had drunken last night between his teeth.

He feels the warm breasts of the woman in his veins;
At once he lashes a little prayer over his pain.
Toward the end of his trial he hopes
To return to the bar where the woman
Always has a leg, raised to the eye.
The beer offers him an identical thought in one look;
Two bandits are refuting the calm logic in his mind;
To whip the horse upon
Which the woman has ascended heaven or to wait for her in hell.

Assorted love on the counter speaking of lipsticks and liquor
In absolute plate laid at the foot of man; he staggers
In thought because he is touched by two liquors;
And for this reason his prayer has become even noisier.
A rabid dog is backing in his sonorous speech.

The man has put on a jacket and the door ahead of him
Has opened to his quick ambition, to walk in the dark, and leave.
He walks through the door as a man and comes
Out as a child of exile. Full of hunger, he searches
For the signature of the desert
To remember the sex he never had the night it was jumping
All over him; to forget the beer that came too heavily

The Art of the Lonely Wanderer

Upon his brow. But the desert too is unstable,
Suffering from a Mediterranean thirst.

In the dark, alone, and thinking about his polygamous anger,
Leaving behind the instant door, the woman, full of beer,
Is probably calling him by the sea of her desert.
But how can he return
To a door he rejected a while ago?
In the wilderness, he edges
The rivers of fire beside his own low ladder.
He mourns the absence of beer and offers a prayer
Between his teeth. His tongue lacks any biblical taste
But his sorrow has a way of dragging him to the fringes
Of the bay where, tonight, he swears to keep his two lovers
Apart from each other. The night is unleashing a cane
And the vagabond is kneeling low.

Gbanabom Hallowell

THE RIVER RUNS BESIDE MY HOUSE

Antiquity runs in the company of silent waters.
It passes by with a migrating ambition; so even
From the back of the palm of the retired century
It holds futuristic assemblies.

The river runs beside my house opposite its miserable song.
A crew is on its waters going after its intellect, canoe after canoe,
The music of the sea loses its song in the high tide.
But no August has ever taken a break to look for its lenses.
So, even if convulsively, the journey cannot be aborted.
The canoes must develop an accent commensurate to the river.

Beside my house the river is sweating,
Sweating from not being a perfect analogy to its migration;
Not being able to leave at anytime the day passes by in its closure.

The river cannot budge from its horizontal obligation.
Its statue is good for the sailor, who
By his sword shall call to violence
Wherever it is climbing the sadness of the vertical man.

My house is shaken by the river; therefore,
I wake up in my manhood
To dress at dawn when the distant journey signals its migration.
I must leave by the next river in the hour of the clock.
I must leave to go where it tires its wings,
Where the tenth canoe is not known by any headcount.

A man is standing by my house today
Waiting for the final river to tell his story.
But river after river the truth about his

The Art of the Lonely Wanderer

Insincerity surfaces in the horizon.
Who waits for river ending to tell his story?
The man has been declared to have an opaque relationship
With the bank of the river; he sits on it with the mind of an impala.
The bank is bare with a rough soul.
Beside the river the man with a story to tell stands baptismally
With two pillars to his listening ears.
He is consoled by his own wretchedness,
Waiting for the hour at which to jump in the river,
To preach his story to whomever wants to listen.
But the river is unrepentant,
Coming along with children wailing for them to be taken away
With children passing me by my house

I SEE DEATH LEAVING BY THE BACK DOOR

There goes Wotho, the street lover, with death under her armpit.
Two severe minds go into an empty space
Under her control, a grave of morsel,
New-born death wakes young in its life
In the soft body of the dead.
It lays healthy, pure of life in a death inspired pain.

Who goes there, beside death, alive!

Solemn following, the leadership of death is blunt;
Philosophical caravan,
Death goes on tiptoe in the company of its disciples
Named in twelve candid coffins.

Who goes there in death, alive!

Look between the yellow flowers, what sentiment
Is throbbing underneath
The petals of life?
What is sinking below its knees in suspicious ending,
Taking into itself the green breath of flowers?

In the bones of the jackass, death is leaving by the backdoor!

A little while ago, the sick man walked
In and after an herbal attention
The body that stood erect in its vertical
Manhood turned out
To be the production element of the soft flesh of death.
Whose dress is under the sad foil!

The Art of the Lonely Wanderer

In the neighborhood two shoulders fell under last night.
By the morning a bird announced
The arrival of an influential hazard;
Before long the backdoor is accessing the life of death.

A monster is soft upon the cold slab!

Death has an anxious mouth, one given to death mine.
Its teeth is naked in hiding, acting with a liquid mind,
Wet in thought and soaked in its strokes.

In what battlefield did it fall, the brother of death!

The other death, the digital brother, as much a twin self?
Who battled in the wake of the century that brought
Them to life? That gave it a better weapon?
It's now clear why the analogue brother is fiercest;
It's for this brother, the death of death, alive!

THE HOUR IS ABOUT TO COME

At once, the entire book opens in only one page
Bringing alive the last drum and the *tum tum*
Of the voodoo belt, the briefcase with the tiny button
Inside, to fit the shirt for the sake of the breastbone.

Put on more human heat if the fan has no electricity,
Put on your heat and stand on your sweat; let the remainder
Anxiety burn with your farts—the water is washing itself
In the final river in readiness of the cleansing of the elbow
Of time, twisting itself between two decades.

The hour is about to come with little tender minutes
And second seconds that never wanted to be first.
Brother, prophesies are urinating their malarial truths.
I say comrades, did you check the wall clock before washing
Your faces? Did you cry before their dutifulness, their
Prompt acceptance of an arrival?

Comrades, brothers, whoever you are in this grand finale,
We are all standing on a posthumous ground.
Throw your eyes where you cast your gaze,
And do not look down where the dust is nothing but dust

Where is that man who cried about Africa three times in his sleep?
Where is the hand of the continent with which he woke up?
He spoke to us this morning in an African way,
Talking about an hour stuck somewhere in his eye.
A book of a thousand pages today opens in only one page
And a restless drum booms with voodoo legs
There is a heaven in the hour belching hell.
There is a book at the end of the hour's curve.

The Art of the Lonely Wanderer

A little pin is aiming to prick the eye of the hour.
The hour, comrades, the hour comes, bringing itself effectively.

Where you not warned in your own accent
That the hour shall come when the hour shall come?
Get up and take your painkillers through your nose;
Soften your body with your sacred heart.
If you have need for a surgeon, go to a physician;
If you need to talk to a lawyer, seek a judge.
Go ahead of yourself, legally
And stand on your sweat, medically.

Listen to the voodoo coming from your soul.
The hour is about to come, instantly
With an archaeological temper, ugly from a distant lamp.
Throw open your windows and your doors,
Forsake your meanwhile where you un-roof your head.
Withdraw your hands from your pockets
And pay attention to the clock
Because when it strikes, the hour would have arrived, impatiently.

ROLLING STONE

Rolling stone, a bullet is set against your tomorrow
Rolling stone, a pan is beating down the syndrome of pain
Rolling stone, a gentle summer is beating hard on its season
Rolling stone, a moss is divided twice beside your between territory
Rolling stone, a tribute is on your wandering
Rolling stone, a category of migrants hold their souls for life

Rolling stone, mankind seeks what cannot be sought after
Rolling stone, a narrative going down the road alone
Rolling stone, solitude is alone walking into a crowd
Rolling stone, a man is leaving by the energy of his belt
Rolling stone, two babies are returning through the sea (how sad)
Rolling stone, the persuasion is cooler than the temper

Rolling stone, one door is quicker than the other
Rolling stone, a beggar has become rich by begging from the poor
Rolling stone, a man goes into himself before his name
Rolling stone, ten of two men wander believing they have long left
Rolling stone, the poems go ahead of the poet in verses
Rolling stone, tonight a distant traveler is changing his course

Rolling stone, two apples shall fall from a tree in different suits
Rolling stone, a fellow remains blind, not in the eyes
Rolling stone, after the gamble the man won his little finger and left
Rolling stone, two shall move a million to leave their wealth behind
Rolling stone, the hour returned as a minute, leaving as a second
Rolling stone, the table looks for a chair until the dinner goes cold

Rolling stone, suicide is no longer news in the papers
Rolling stone, a lean man is escaping between two sorrows
Rolling stone, one shall become president and two shall flee

The Art of the Lonely Wanderer

Rolling stone, the rider has passed his stop leaving behind his head
Rolling stone, liberty has left with a pair of slaves
Rolling stone, seven no longer stays behind because of seven

Rolling stone, a man argues that he had died long ago
Rolling stone, a woman was the absence of her presence
Rolling stone, a vulture is scavenging the body of his own carcass
Rolling stone, the end of man is determined by the road length
Rolling stone, a long pause always waits for the urgent wanderer
Rolling stone, silence has gone between us with a cap on its head

Gbanabom Hallowell

A MAN IS MOVING AROUND IN MY HEAD

A Man is moving around in my head in the form of a theory,
Hitting against everything on his way, kicking even
The perimeter holding on to my sanity when I'm drunk.
I hate the scattered notes coming out of the theory
Each time it rotates my head, but the doctor
Said it's an influenza that came in through my eyes
Looking for a host to lay its dirty eggs on.

Years ago, a rational migraine sat in one corner of my head
Waiting for them who came with knives and sticks; but alas,
It has lost its own head and now like a fool it has
Become the migraine it was supposed to be after meeting
With the man who is in my head in the form of a theory.

I'm thinking, any idiot can be a theory, living
Off of the vexatious moments of one's head beside
Any migraine that was born to explode, kill its host
And then, itself, becoming bodiless tooth in dire need
To survive in the emptiness of a dead man's future
Full of odor and of rotten agenda.

What feminine feeling has come over me that I must
Think a masculine threat against my own person,
Holding on to a shadow of steel being forced into my head
By the very hour that returns again and again with bad memories?
In my head an urgent thought is wrestling with the human theory
And rapid voices duel with each other in academic agony.

Anastasia was one theory that poured burnt oil in my brain
Then came Kumba, a localized theory, with all her sub-theories,
Promising happiness as the concept of her looking eyes.

The Art of the Lonely Wanderer

Here comes an unfathomable theory, an abstract man
With a pistol in his mouth, in his own hand,
Shouting for liberation,
Pissing in my brain, seeking to be read as he appears,
In pages, flipping over cover to cover, making a point
As noisy as a tight thunder that blows off his eardrums.

It is time to make that long journey between my head
And the city outside, to read all those books from afar
While I establish that a rage is in my hands, weeping
From being unable to hold on to the argument within
its reach, a rage that knows all the theories by name
and yet cannot make a call to any prospective one.

Gbanabom Hallowell

LIBERTY LEFT WITH A PAIR OF SLAVES

Liberty stood on the legs of a pair of slaves and
Pushed a fist in the air, claiming the victory of the sweat.
The plantation has come down to the table fruits,
A dinner, full of knives and other cutleries smear
Of blood without the hunters ever showing up.
The courageous chains that dragged the ruthless years of the ape
From the harbor of the foxes to the hatred of the wolves
Brought smoke in the eyes of the bereaved under the versatile
 Theft of the priests of hoods and the veils of prayers.

Freedom remains castrated in the conquistador's emblem;
Liberty came down in dust in the eyes of the mourners,
Touching on the flabby breasts of the widow of pain.
O liberty, your visibility is a scandal in suffocated throats,
As you seek conquest in the beggar's shoes.
You blow off in ecstasy in the barn of the widowed breasts,
Singing freedom through your teeth
While the black slave was still in the mines breathing toxic gas.
Pull back your hand from the lungs of the wind!

Liberty, tonight you have left victory behind, while you
Hold hostage a pair of slaves, a pair of their identity,
Fleeing from justice; the smoke of your freedom burns
With ideological fraud; across from the distance with your nemesis,
Wherever you are tonight, the incredible slave remains free
In his slavery, remains healed in his pains, remains
Rich in his poverty; remains happy in his sadness,
Remains hopeful in his despair; remains alive in his death,
Because Liberty, your liberty has no freedom, the God of the poor!

The Art of the Lonely Wanderer

Absolute liberty, Africa is tired of your betrayal, your
Too much bad flesh against your skin. You betrayed
The miner in the pit while holding his Sunday pay in the form
Of a cheque; little freedom, your immensity speaks little,
To the heart of the slave whose theoretic eyes
Kill the ancient patience of the caged bird.
After years of slavery, after the capital interest of the African
Slave posted zero in Wall Market,
In the eyes of his conquistador, it shouldn't be a fraudulent liberty
To walk in sadly on him with a bad leg.

Liberty, you are busted! End of code to your name.
Come from the flowers of your lust and surrender your rot;
Freedom shall seek you out in the foxes of your liberty.
You shall be hounded to the pen of your voice.
What liberty runs away with the freedom
We seek in our human pockets?
Who goes into freedom through liberty
Without a human autonomy? Freedom, take away
Your slave from the thieving hands of liberty!

MY WINGS ARE MEANT TO FLY

The morning man opened the chicken shed.
The domestic bird
Took a restrictive flight, picked up the floor!
Stuck on the clock.
The hour embraced its feathers.
The wild bird flapped, spreads its plumages
And domesticated its head—headed for the big yard.
For the home
Bird a distance is suffering between a flight and a walk—
A perching bird,
Mostly, of restrictive height—the sky always daring higher.
The house bird
Never budging higher than a pick of the beak.
Who can conquer self
Twice in the year to make a record higher than last year's?
Who can keep striving to ascend closer to the sun?
All anyone can do is beat self once,
Maybe twice and settle for that victory; for the soft

Side of the victory. An African red ribbon ties
The chicken-bird to ceremony,
To sacrifice, to three firestones of voodoo.
A man is in blood all over beside
The slain sheep, the slain white sheep.
The truth is revealed: a rooster is crying
Out of its wings, the corner bird is taking the center branch.
The tree is falling
To rise, to hold its Apex against its branches.
Who wants to fly toward the sun?
Who wants to hold a feather to a wing?
A feather and a wing across the impossible

The Art of the Lonely Wanderer

Miles of the sky.
Friendly skies are holding a thousand birds by their gravities;
By the naked gravity of each its solar, the wings flap.
Then up from
Below the impossible there is a domesticated
Hen crying for the chicken-bird;
The sky has voodoo in its land
Stretched from the sky-path where Africa

Begins to map to the tip of its Sahara
Where the land is still black at sunup
And the people wanting to fly are black to their skins.
The birds of the people flock
To fly; their wings are made to fly.
A priority comes with hope each time a leader turns into a bird.
They come who want to fly to deny; who want to fly to argue;
They come who want to fly to apply;
They come who want to fly to confess; and truth
Always slaps the face of hope with feathers,
And the calamity of the domesticated
Hen grows into sadness.
There is no transformation here; you have to bear fruits
Of flying nature, of the creed of feathers speaking
Truth to birds, of man hoping
To fly because he has hands of wings.
A feather, a plumage and a wing to dare the front,
There, where the journey sustains!

Gbanabom Hallowell

A SOLITARY BIRD FLIES THE SKY

From above the tip of the apple front,
A bird spreads its wings peripherally;
Taking a flight from the cardinal south,
It allows the firmament's four
Cardinals to its own point, sustaining
Its solitary confinement against
The sphere without.
Latitudinal and upfront, it paints the sky
With a lazy brush, leaving a rainbow behind.
The bird is calm,
Much to its own loneliness, it is silent, a little to its own loud wings.
Subject to its aim, the flight remains focused on solitude.

The right to its cloud pushes the bird
To a lazy wind, so below the cloud
Of its sail, the sky takes into blue waters;
And unto the experience of levels
Of condition to which it could ascend,
The bird sits on a pouch of wind.
Then in favor of its advantage,
It takes off as if landing on a mantle of cloud.
To its amazement the cloud loses its architecture
And sits upon itself in layers.
So, in an utter speed, the bird aims for the palace;
Bringing forth a sorrow
On its brow, lamenting the short-lived
Infrastructure of the clouds in the sky.
O that the clouds where made of steel!
On a day like this, the bird soars terrestrially with vigilance,
To compose a brain with a signature applauding the gravity,
Guarding its audacity to hold time outside of its alarm.

The Art of the Lonely Wanderer

Today the bird is in the air approaching the wind; it is in the cloud
Approaching it where it is grey and where its serenity speaks
Of the season of the waters.
Four points of cardinal interests, the bird remains conscious
Of the clouds' flowery presence: its points of emergence,
Its points of flights and of arrival;
The tuxedo clouds in line against the somber sky.

The sky is not deaf to the lonely wanderer, many
Of its favorite songs beyond
Forgetting, have come from birds; from celestial
Migrants off to Blueland; alas!
The canoes are capsizing below the astronomy
Of the clouds.
But today the marine layer lies on the romantic edges of the sphere.
Up above the sky a lonely bird is wandering,
Spreading its plumages across the heavens,
And an angel taking stock.
What poet wouldn't want to be a bird to fly the sky
While angels, from their boreholes watch, wandering,
And wonder at the wandering
At the edge of instant lightning?

Gbanabom Hallowell

WHEN THE VULTURE TAKES ITS FLIGHT

When the vulture takes its flight it spreads it across the sky.
It builds a road
In the wind with trust in the air.
The sky maybe a vast expanse yet
The vulture knows the way to scavenge and it knows
Where to relax; where
The tide is low and where the tide is high.
The vulture is an apparent bird that

Sways its plumages to take in the blue of the sky
With verve and keep it firm.
It flails its feathers, circumspect of grey tension.
To determine it's wandering,
One must follow its eyes, those restless balls,
And one would know the horizons that come
Into view. The vulture peers between trees and branches,
Holding a breath in its throat.

The vulture only sinks below where a bloodless
Child has died, where a healthy bull
will shed its blood for the kingdom.
With a gentle roughness it long ago traded its hands
For two dark claws.
Without a shadow.
It is itself a shadow and has learned to creep
Behind the dead.
The vulture is a blatant bird, with
An exotic taste, forever patient.
The vulture, a planetary bird oscillates between
Its hunger and the faggots of dead
Meats. After the vulture has mapped

The Art of the Lonely Wanderer

Its path for the day, it spreads unto occasional
Branches to assess the watermark in the middle
Of its hope and the hope of its calm
Anger, running impatiently as hunger-tides.
No vulture has a song in its head

Like other peripheral birds do,
Roaming the sky with the aimless desire to seek
The ointment of the stars and the unknown world.
The vulture is a black star
In the sky, fetching prominence for itself,
So that when a beast of no nation dies
Below at the bottom, the road shall become shorter to ply.
O bald headed vulture,

Hunch in the sky, divide your time between blue shades;
Join the kettle and wander
About the adult distance where you shall never age.
Spread your wings, the heat
Is following your smell like a long line of lightening .
The vulture reveres in its alternative
Other, and each time it sinks below the level of its flight,
It falls below the waist of its carnivore.

In the scavenging world of the vulture, the volt is large
Enough for more kinds; therefore,
Descending, claw by claw, the vulture becomes a committee;
From the distance above
It lands with a patient calm.
You have heard it said that the vulture is a patient bird, and
It must be added that because it knows how to appreciate
The unwanted, the carcass of the world.

I GOT MY THINGS AND LEFT

*"I got my things and left. The sun was coming up.
I couldn't think where to go. I wandered towards
the beer-hall but stopped at the bottle-store where I bought a beer".*
                                        Dambudzo Marechera

In one prolific instance, I got my things alcoholically,
Gathered them where the cemetery was loneliest, and against
The landlord's proximity, I walked up to the bullet bag
In which I existed momentarily.

I remember it all as an opponent portrait to me, lying
Beside Great-ness after it fell from the clock for lack of time.
A stick came between us and I grabbed it because my things
Were packed where I had gotten them.

At once I was no longer an alien to the little child who dared
To steal my alcohol when it was most whet for my appetite;
I had to approach my decision with a universal accent
Because now that I had packed I was suddenly
Without a belonging.

Another memory doubled its steps into my head by the suspended
Door and met with a priest who was shying away from my bottles
With an instant action of goodness anointed in human corrective
Measure. For a man made up to leave, that was a luggage indeed.

In confidence, there was the room I left in all sanity and
The sincerity between us both, in which I was not to be trusted
With living quietly beside my body and not touch it with a voodoo
Of mind after I had been filled with rage by the ocean bottle.
My room was blind to my plans though it held so much truth

The Art of the Lonely Wanderer

About my resolve; the roof was coming
Down on me like a landlord,
And in that instant the room was as spontaneous
As I was in the hour leading up to my signature
In the tomb of time.

I deserved an ovation; every drunkard goes through sanity, before
A hundred solitudes is evicted from the throat of any Darwinian
Fossil, threatening a come back to the imagination of our scientists
Who have melted every slogan uttered by God
In the centuries before us.

I left here before I ever came back drawn to the bottle store;
Alcohol left too. The green followed after its bottle
And the liquor before its beverage.
The perimeter around where I picked up my soul was the place
The philosopher blessed the journey in the portrait with a first step.

AFTER THE UNIVERSAL ROMEO HAD DIED

After the universal Romeo had died with the capital love of Verona
That city inflicted itself with a generous hunger of violent delights;
Cesar came to love Rome through the Venetian nights that
Dropped on Verona, exceeding themselves
In the whistling sound, shedding slickly
Across Cupid's plot at the dining table
Of exorbitant Roman affection.

What merit of love killed Romeo universally,
Making humanimals benefit
From the narrative kiss of history?
Did Romeo invent love or the relational
Steel that made it oppose to death?
He died in flowers where Juliet fell
As a bud.
Two hearts in the longing river, longing to flow; shadowy
River, flowing universally black, universally African.

Ethiopia was stabbed with a Roman sword in the year
Of the monotonous war
When Italy came to Africa with a general's mind;
Ethiopia fought back
The emblem of the West but touched the tip of the sword
With a love-tongue.
That night, Romeo and Juliet roamed
Africa in the pair of their universal love,
The Montague-Capulet tragedy came to the continent
With a fluent narrative.
Othello flew to Venice on a broom and for his dark skin,
The Senate listened to his being accused of witchcraft
Love for Desdemona. On Cupid's oath

The Art of the Lonely Wanderer

Desdemona broke the African spell and learned
To love Othello again
Through a European voodoo.
Othello became the universal moor of love.
His tigress saved his day from the blood
In Iago's quick sword of friendship.

Universal Romeo! Two lovers remained perished
In affection for each other.
A sword kept the torrent between their bleeding hearts.
In suicidal affection their love shouted against the silent
Organ of their throats.
The hour of love honored the seconds
Spent in waking a sleeping Juliet.
The body waited in death for love to touch
A hand on the cheeks of trust.

Pushkin had the ordinary sorrow of being born black
In Russia, brother
To the moor. Serpent of the color of thirst, he was a man with
An enormous love and a big eye for poetry shaped in the blonde
Of his black looks;
Romeo gave him a hand for sword and a pen for love,
Then by his own want, he took the heart
Of Othello and swallowed it whole.

A tenth of Romeo is doing the affection.
The ultimate power of love,
The bandana desire, the two happiness in one,
That universal story in which
Juliet died creatively and together with Romeo,
Emerged as sphinxes is walking,
Swimming and flying, catching up with the truth

That Romeo was in a way
A dark lover in shadows, below the pillars
Of thirst for the love of the blonde.

The Art of the Lonely Wanderer

WHERE DOES ETERNITY GO FROM HERE?

Eternity is a child of collusion, the accidental blood brother
Rejecting itself, utterly coaxial; ultimate hot piece, going cold
In warm condition, everlasting fever in the audacity of the years,
In millennium wandering, in millennium circumstances;
An element full of life when it is wasting in view.
Coming alive in my brother who died while protecting himself,
Alive in the lifeless body of the bird who fell from the sky;
The beggar's last breath has eternity waiting to be born;
The wounded snake unable to ooze a poison, has eternity
On its head flailing.

The perfect tongue of the guanaco has eternity in the flesh,
The brutal beast with eternity in the eye,
The raging sea is tormented by eternity;
The crustacean blue is red with eternity.
The road disappears with it at the bend.
The dead man's eyes, with a plot of hope, shut their orbs.
The plaque of truth is still in the breath of eternal silence.
There is an eleventh hour in the plasma puking eternity,
Stopping which clock?

The endless flight is in limbo, falling off what sky?
The drawl of pain its eternity.
A coin in the hand of the beggar has the eternity of the rich;
The speed of a motor engine is the eternity of the car;
The aggression of the office worker is the eternity of his bladder
When it lies under the eye of the surgeon.
The surgeon is his own eternity laid as tears
In the eyes of the mother,
The sister who also is a mother of the brother.
The sister is the lover of the man who will bring eternity

To lie on the breasts of her womb.
The fruitful womb has an eternity equal
To that of the fruitless womb;
The barren child has as much eternity as the child
With a natal day to celebrate.

Officially speaking, then, where does eternity go from here?
After it frees itself from the beggar's torment, after the brother
Has fled from his own soul; after the snake has bruised its head;
After the woman has suffered the pains?
To what soul does eternity relate to; under what pressure does
It visit its victims?
What organic instrument does eternity operate on, to come
And go beside the tragedy of rivers flowing? In the circle of what
Compromise does eternity leave its abode to rest in peace?

WHEN THE SOLDIER GOES TO WAR

He goes sacredly in the armored company of other dead officers
To kill the living enemy deployed below a tomb; he goes among
The ghosts of war sent by leaders picking cotton under tables.
A bullet from the enemy;
A bullet to the enemy.
The smell of cemetery comes to his nose after
Kissing his wife goodbye. He sweats
In his boots conspiratorially.

A severe enemy is deployed in the abrupt quietness,
Keeping a heart just above his gun, above his death,
Wounded already in his little boxes, a mantle waits in his heart.

A book of war is missing in his chest retrieved in guns; tablet, you
Wonder what piece of window falls shattered on idols of war,
Killing coward soldiers in bravery; comrade in arms the city library
Is under attack in seven domains where the ring smelted itself.

Bow to the low temperature if a command goes through
The General's ears. The game of war is dancing in his eyes;
The sergeant should die if the lame must
Walk to touch the barrel of the gun.

But it is the young man almost falling into shadows
Eighty eight days in pain
A soldier falls into twelve shadows waiting to go into first battle.
A future man is dying yesterday in ancient fashion leaving a wife
Behind with tears; but the gun has answered to the man.
To war he goes, his teeth ahead of him; his finger nails crouching
The rocks of the air….stentorian foreground…..
The soldier is disheveled

Gbanabom Hallowell

On behalf of his family and his youthful opacity.
The blood has cuddled
And the man in the inside has yelled to the man
In green fatigue.
A bullet from the enemy;
A bullet to the enemy.
The smell of cemetery comes to his nose after
Kissing his wife goodbye. He sweats
In his boots conspiratorially.

Comrades in arms…..and against arms
In velvet towel the gun grows, in pure white….
Kiss the butt O soldier.
Kiss it beside the cheeks of his wife, beside the smile of his young.
Kiss it beside the flag and beside the republic;
Kiss it against the metaphor coiling in his heart.

OF HUNTERS AND GATHERERS

Manufacturing survival….
Clear the pathways for the hunger
The strangled prey
From last night struggling
To budge in raw air
Along the gatherer's hope.

Make, create and innovate
Archeologically
To gather the gains of Wall Street.
Dismantle the old statute;
Begin with the image,
Follow up with the Panama Papers;
Go hunt and gather far away…..

Hunt for God's yam
Not touched before.
Scavenge in sea shore,
The barracuda could
Just be warming up in the sun;
Follow after the long dynamic
Street culture,
Contextualize in formal codes.

The hunters and the gatherers
Take the ocean by the river,
Aiming to shore up stream
With folios of the World Bank.
They go after bread
But are faced
With the plenitude of flour.

Today the hunters'
Tool is ahead of them,
Digging up
The fruits of the mouth.

The hunters' aggressive
Tongue tasting sweet,
The tongue of the hunter
Licks the gatherer's hands;
The tongue in between,
The quickness of its draw,
Its red heart dances in the lonely palate.

A ROUGH PAIR OF SANDALS ON THE SIDEWALK

Tired, confidence broke in the middle;
The sandals and their skins, the steps and their prints;
Bronchitis, the pit came up with its phlegm;
In league with testimonial miles of fed eyes,
Sandals, sweating the man, sandals to wear,
To walk and to work….

Sincerely, sandals of miles to go,
Miles left like thoughts of air, fleeing the mind
That invented it; chasing after grandchildren
In nearby trees.

Sandals holding firm to love, to friendship, agriculturally;
Crushing the pain of fabric; life out of stones,
And water the level the road meets the sole via the sandals.

A man wore sandals and roamed
The desert for forty days and nights
Pleading the cause of other men,
Appealing to God only in sandals.
Favored footwear walk the wandering
Of man among the nations of beasts.
Divine sandals; stay tempted in the desert because
There you have got your wit….you listened to the wind
When the evildoer crossed over from the right to the shadows
Of the left. You called out to the divine
Man, you carried to watch out.
You heard him in outcry:

Man must not live on bread alone!

You took the bread in your fist by the entrance of your mouth
And kicked it behind the man, the divine skin;
Then you took the man away on to a pinnacle, but the baker
Was locked in the evildoer and followed you, O sandals!

You serve man; you serve the foot of man.
In the immense bulk of his wandering, you serve.
He covers the miles in thoughts and drops their pressures on you.
You take the toe by its twitching and make the owner
Tick at the top of his head; you calm the heart through
The tender soles that itch for a walk.

O Sandals! O pair!
Right here on the sidewalk you come to your grief,
Demolished.

Where is man?

HAVE YOU LOST YOUR MIND?

Ladies and Gentlemen,
After this examination is taken and returned to the books,
After the mind keeper and the mind are reconciled,
The jury shall attend to the mortal varsity
Of the soul to pass judgment.
In the event that the mind is no longer in love with the body
Shall it consult with the spirit of man?

Today a child opens an umbrella as the first effort
Of its growing bones; the day has not fallen over the earth
But it is okay if a child and its mind are minding their business
In the true state of the life between the two of them.

A man lives because his mind lives; the day is open
To a free mind and without waiting for a pair of legs
The mind can wander without the man; the mind
Must have a day to itself to mind its own business,
To be solvent before the dark takes over the sum.

Have you lost your mind, Wallace Johnson?
In how many voices did you grow up in?
Bai Bureh, have you lost your mind?
Why did you burn the tax documents in the thatch house?
The colonialists are coming at your door with the traitor brother.
The conquistador will kill you where he murdered you, tribally.

He lost his mind who solved the anger of the mob
He lost his mind who took to the street in yellow flames
He lost his mind who embraced the sea when it was only a river
He lost his mind coming back to back with his conscience
He lost his mind who battled before the war began

He lost his mind who dared to admit that.

I hear a tooth aching in his dumb mouth
There is a dark broom in the room
The terrorist shot down the plane
The Caribbean voodoo took the mind of the dictator into its dull
In the experience, the heart has learned to be lonely
In the presence of its mind
Sadly, the man lost his mind between thoughts
Ladies and Gentlemen,
Speaking in the true sense of a Sierra Leonean,
And remembering all we have gone through as a nation,
After this examination is taken and returned to the books,
After the mind keeper and the mind are reconciled,
The jury shall attend to the mortal varsity
Of the soul to pass judgment.
In the event that the mind is no longer in love with the body
Shall it consult with the spirit of man?

THE NAKED WOMAN GOES IN THE NUDE

There she goes, and after being naked all her youth,
She is suddenly adorned, suddenly dressed in nudity.
No longer naked, she has put on an expensive,
State of the art nudity, Magisterial.
She goes between the ropes,
Coming from being naked to being nude.
She goes terrestrially through the media with hope
That the rope will not come to an end
Already gone ahead of her.

This afternoon a woman goes through my eyes,
After bathing
In a blue river. Instructor of water, the woman
Comes as a river, bringing her lessons out of it, in dry tablets.
She is in the nude, emerging as a fashion designer,
Instructing in the ethics of the sea.

Barracuda woman, coming unto her own undersea
With a happy shroud hanging on her little finger.
She brings the sea by its conscience and the waves
By their clothes.
She is that shark turning her belly
Forty eight times in a minute.
The sea calms before her nudity.

Up from the mines she emerges
With the fingers of the miners on her plain skin;
Their sweats are on her body with
A language closer to peace;
Closer to the middle spirit
Of it all she descends with victory.

There is victory in her taste, in her watery mouth.

Tonight she goes through the still
Hour of the dark.
Her naked body covered
With designer nudity.
She leaps like a wanderer, chasing
After the elusive wind.
Tall in her innocence, she dreams of umbrellas,
She dreams of tall rains coming down in full on her;
She dreams of herself dreaming in the rain
And of ascending the river as if rising unto a hill.
But above all, she dreams of her body coming against its kind…

APPROACHING DEATH
FROM ANOTHER MAN'S EYES

The logic of one man dying from another man's eyes
Carries with it the cruellest drama of despair; a prayer comes
Between the teeth of those eyes even not hoping for an answer;
Death comes on slowly with a jacket of nails.

A dying man lies across the heart of another; a corridor
Goes through between them for the freedom of the two.
A quick eye looks below a lazy one; any minute, the visitor
Will knock on the door with a cold hand.
Any minute….any minute…

The end comes superficially, licking the foam
On the borders of the lips; it comes as a current of lightning
Visible only to the eyes of the other.

When the hour shakes in its presence, the eyes of the other
Winks weakly, there where death approaches the man
Who approaches it; they approach each other philosophically
And share a hug where there is no friendship.
Toward that eternal disposition, smoke gets in the eyes
Of the man who looks to confirm the immensity
Of death coming with a lazy persistence to honor the day!

The eyes of the other are reflecting the Sunday hour,
The prayer of servitude in the lips of the dying man, the cognitive
Widening of the fresh door of odor, of decay in the new suit,
And finally the blinking of his eyes after the hour shall have gone
Away with the swift vanishing of its melancholy.

But the instances come to pass too slowly;
The guitar of sorrow plays its jazz too lightly, following
After the lyre which must rescue its notes from the antiquities
To sound the believable doxology and canticles to God for killing
The man with a hand of duty.

It is finished!
A story has gone missing between his eyes
The governance of his flesh is lost in the world's care.
Two wombs are closing against the mother's pain.
Too much foam in his mouth. His tongue is dancing no more.
The god of taste is gone from him. Life is nothing but taste.
No salt will lie on his tongue to waste to the body of man.
His eyes are broken; they no longer look to see!

THE FUTURE OF STONE

> *Go inside a stone*
> *That would be my way.*
> *Let somebody else become a dove*
> *Or gnash with a tiger's tooth.*
> *I am happy to be a stone.*
>   -Charles Simic

Throw a stone into the future
And you will see it leap with confidence.
Stone belongs to the future.
Its temperament is permanent
Ahead of its waiting.
From its life as a pebble,
A stone is calm in the middle;
For that matter, it can sit still while
Waiting for a single mile.
Knock unto a stone and wait for an answer.
The wind knows the language
That keeps the stone silent.
An audacity of its own future.

The stone is not all hard,
It has a joke of softness,
A sedimentary gentleness.
Fourteen pounds to its being,
The stone is absolute.
Solitary rock, soft core,
The heart beats well in the cyst, in the core.
Its everlasting patience lies
Outside around its hard body
Waiting in breath and the order of the wind

Unto its majestic singleness
Lies the trust of the earth;
The stone marches from pebble to rock,
From rock to hill,
Rolling a million times
Unto its desire to form into a mountain
The future of stone is now, flat on the truth of man!
The Everest is a stone and so is the Kilimanjaro,
The stone stands with a steel of defiance to wander forever!

A PRAYER FOR THE GLOBAL WANDERER

Continental man, your global map
Poses little tiny questions in my head; but you do not
Look like a question mark to me.
You are like a comma,
Not willing to stop the waters
Of the sea under your legs.
Unconditional voyager, Gulliver
Will envy your travels.
The cardinals have put four points on your head.
Of Gulliver we celebrated in the passive, but of you
We multiply the persons of many people to pass
A fierce mile against a lion
In honor of your name.
In Bafordia, we said *aha aha* several times
Before the priests of Aragon
Gave thanks for seeing access to water.

Your famous forgetting of the stars does not take away
From your knowledge of the places you have instrumentally
Tied your love to—the Casablanca of waiting miles,
The Cairo sticks tied to your warm bread—
Ouagadougou,
Where you assisted yourself to be a man of journeys;
To the Gaza Strip, where you spoke seven languages against
Your citizenship of all combined—
And to Palestine,
Where your love for Christ situated itself implacably.

True to your voyage, every journey
Has come back in favor of you.
Accordion Europe took the sensitivity of your steps

With warm regards.
Among the Romans,
You stood evidently supportive of the Italians
When Rome unsuccessfully tried
To withdraw its city from Italy.
You saw the big names of Athens
Threatened by the Persian Gulf
And that what remained of Germany
After Hitler was a country of bunkers
Built to eternally hide from the fear of Hitler.
Otto Von Bismarck, with a Prussian
Attitude stood the African sun still
Until the continent
Dropped into thousands of urchins.

MEET ME WHEREVER YOU FIND ME

And finally I leave with
an occasional mind
Having waited intensely
for your cognitive order;
I was told you always
come as a shadow
where the lights
Celebrate themselves.

In short, you never ever arrive.
You linger for long in the air.
You linger in motion
You linger in sound,
Saying your name aloud
In two syllables
Among the green grasses
Turned yellow in anger?

Come with me if I must say.
Turn your coat toward the darker
Side, where the shadow
Lives longer;
Spread an apple
Ahead of the devil's
Appetite and follow it
With a penultimate
Choice of ultimatum.

To what numeracy
Should our numbers
Be counted? With What flour

Will you bake the bread tonight?
I am leaving the house
And by night I shall be among the goers.
The night's little voices shall send me off.
Apportion the road to the walkers of the night
And let the hours follow our steps.

The brother is waiting for the man
Beside his own brother; beside the truth
Of waiting there lies a man whose
Brother lives with him.
Therefore, meet me this day
Wherever you find me. Among
The bulrushes there waits an object
That must be met where anyone finds it.
Tomorrow when the day dawns,
I shall become that object!

THE ART OF THE LONELY WANDERER

Comrade of the road, I have been following
Your travails, your mind, approaching your art.
Connoisseur, move your body by your conscience;
Alone in your arm
You dare the road, the combustible and the agricultural.
Quantitative man, your body is listening to the too many pains
Walking down your legs,
Having wandered from one pole to another
In metric distance.
Your bull is urgent on the road, substantially;
Your chemical mind of a little stick in your hand has wandered long
With you through the buffalo gesture of your animal challenge.
You wander aesthetically,
Designing the road with a vagrant attitude.
Drunk, the road tosses its body
Reckless of curves around your steps.
What metaphor brings you together in one love?

In this year of the Iguana the road moans in its double irony,
Hiccupping and galloping as it flees
Under the soles of the wanderer.
Contrary to the calculated beats of the progressive leg,
The double enjambments of the road lag
Side by side with broken blades
And free spirits.
Hendecasyllabic man, you put on your sorrow where
Your blood rushes through to your spine so that in journeying
Forward, your brain comes up against the book of flying pages.
On the road the man is besieged beside his thought: a ceremony
In art form. On foot miles, literary of human fields, where diction
Listens to the philosophical soles of the wanderer

To enter his thoughts,
The road lies on its belly with a podium of mind.

The body sweats on the mind of the man
On the road; the road carrying
The man sweats its terracotta mind;
Two minds at work—anacoluthon
 On two independent arguments taking a relationship to the future.
Two images feeding on each other.
Man and road, objects of each other's
Soul in the fandango of an accismus around sublime fantasy.
The road is the personification of the man; the man an hyperbole
Of dusty mind tired by the aimless road
Turning into a path, foot after foot.
The man might ask, "How many steps does it take to be a road?"
The road too might ask, "How many lengths
Does it take to make a man?"
Who can proffer an answer without
Falling for the logic of the philosopher?
Therefore, let the man be a man in his own right.
The last path standing is the road
Therefore, let the road be a road in its own right.
The last mortal standing is the man

Talk of the wanderer on air or at sea meeting controversial waves.
Who wanders more than the waves?
Full of a bandana heart, the waves
Sail across the length of their metaphors
And with precise nothingness
Sail a long jive of change of mind.
Today man takes the horizontal
Wandering because his mind has enslaved him so.
He goes up to touch the cloud and descends with

The forgetfulness of stone.
He goes down below and wriggles
Among the fishes of the bottom deep and emerges
With the forgetfulness of stone. With the remembering of stone
With the forgetfulness of stone. With the remembering of stone
Man wanders everywhere with the remembering of stone; in the
Body of the devices that speak to *the art of the lonely wanderer!*

Gbanabom Hallowell

AFTERWORD

In the early 1990s, as a civil war raged in parts of the country, a budding group of young writers began to meet, once every week, at the United States Information Agency (USIA) in Freetown to read their (unpublished) poems. A military regime, which had seized power with a promise of ending the war quickly, was providing no respite from the ravages of the war. Instead, it had become corrupt and repressive. This state of affairs provided, so to speak, a rallying point for the poets.

Elvis Hallowell, as he was then known, was important in bringing this group together. He was at the time a librarian at the USIA; he certainly helped provide a forum for the group. And he was one of the most promising and distinctive voices in the group. He had a deeply melodious voice, and I thought that he was by far the best poetry reader in the group.

We had become friends at about this time; I remember that it was him who recommended that I read the American novelist Saul Bellow, a winner of the Nobel Prize. He had me take a copy of the book from the library, but I found it a disappointment; I couldn't penetrate Bellow: his experiences were alien to me. I tried Bellow again recently with greater success, but his appeal remains very limited for me.

Sometime in 1994, Hallowell showed me a manuscript of his first poetry collection. It was resonantly entitled *Hills of Temper*. I found it to be a wonder of acute observation and passion. The ongoing war and the distemper of praetorian ineptitude were the background; the poet, un-awed, gave voice to a growing national anxiety. *Hills of Temper* was published in 1996. It still feels fresh and complete and lyrical, the musings of a deeply sensitive and intelligent young soul.

It is a more mature and assured voice that we encounter in *The Art of the Lonely Wanderer*, Hallowell's new collection of 40 poems. 'Elvis' as his first name has been replaced by 'Gbanabomk'; and, somehow, the music of the poems is more attenuated. *The Art of the Lonely Wanderer* is a series of philosophical musings by a poet who, once discussed as promising, is now indisputably a master of the craft.

The Art of the Lonely Wanderer

The poems depict a world of illusions, of the anonymity of ordinary people lost in the maze of global capitalism; the presumed liberty of the poor rendered meaningless in a world dominated by greed and moneyed power. Despair seems to rot society; and the little man's motion of prayer is overpowered by a mind more

set on the woman last night
He couldn't bed than it is on God.
He contemplates sex in the form of a prayer and curses the woman
Under his stained breath. His mind takes a leap and clutches
The beer he had drunken last night between his teeth.

This poem is entitled "Of Sex, Exile and Longing" – but it is far from being louche, as some might hope. It is instead, like many of the poems in this collection, a meditation on what might be called the pathos of betwixt and between, of the crushed aspirations of sensitive people in a world dominated by grosser men with power and money. At least this is how I understand them. The point is that the profundity of Hallowell's thought is expressed in similarly profound ways. When the poet evokes Romeo and Juliet, we expect a meditation on the purity and innocence of love in an extremely adverse situation. There are hints of love al-right; but the meditation takes on race, the great Pushkin (Russian but descended from an Ethiopian), the place of Africa in world history, Rome's forays on the continent (though no Roman conqueror, not even the adventurous Emperor Hadrian, dared as far as Ethiopia).

Universal Romeo! Two lovers remained perished
In affection for each other.
A sword kept the torrent between their bleeding hearts.
In suicidal affection their love shouted against the silent
Organ of their throats.
The hour of love honored the seconds
Spent in waking a sleeping Juliet
The body waited in death for love to touch

A hand on the cheeks of trust.

Pushkin had the ordinary sorrow of being born black
In Russia, brother
To the moor. Serpent of the color of thirst, he was a man with
An enormous love and a big eye for poetry shaped in the blonde
Of his black looks;
Romeo gave him a hand for sword and a pen for love,
Then by his own want, he took the heart
Of Othello and swallowed it whole.

Auden, that most profound of modern poets, said that poetry cannot be effective as a political weapon. "The social and political history of Europe would be what it has been if Dante, Shakespeare, Michelangelo, Mozart, et al., had never lived," he said. A poet, he continued, "*qua* poet, has only one political duty, namely, in his own writing to set an example of the correct use of [language] which is always being corrupted. When words lose their meaning, physical force takes over. By all means, let a poet, if he wants to, write what is now called an 'engagé' poem, so long as he realizes that it is mainly himself who will benefit from it. It will enhance his literary reputation among those who feel the same as he does." But Auden's world – Europe and America – had arrived at their resolution long before he was born; it was very much a settled world, at ease with itself and one which had inflicted itself on other worlds.

Hallowell is writing for and about the world that Auden's world still dominates. He has to be political; and his voice will both give pleasure and instruct. This collection does just that.

Lansana Gbarie, PhD
Author of
- *Dirty War in West Africa: The RUF and the Destruction of Sierra Leone*
- *War, Politics and Justice in West Africa: Essays 2003-2014* (SLWS, 2015)

SIERRA LEONEAN WRITERS SERIES (SLWS)

Focusing on academic, fictional, and scientific writing that will complement other relevant materials used in schools, colleges, universities and other tertiary institutions, the Sierra Leonean Writers Series (SLWS) aims to promote good quality books by Sierra Leoneans writing on any topics and other writers from around the world who write on themes and issues about Sierra Leone.

It is the publisher's hope that students and other readers in Sierra Leone will eventually be at least some of the primary beneficiaries of these works. Not only will people in Sierra Leone be able to read materials that relate to their own lives and experiences, budding writers will also be able to draw inspiration from the efforts of their compatriots and other established writers.

Submitted work undergoes a rigorous peer-review process before being accepted for publication, with an international editorial board providing guidance to writers.

SLWS, based in Warima and Freetown in Sierra Leone, distributes books globally through AMAZON.COM. In Sierra Leone, SLWS books are currently available at the SLWS Bookshop in Warima (near Masiaka) and at CLC Bookshop, 92 Pademba Road in Freetown.

SLWS co-publishes some titles with Karantha Publishers in Sierra Leone.

For further information, please visit our website:
www.sl-writers-series.org
or contact the publisher, Prof. Osman A. Sankoh (Mallam O.) publisher@sl-writers-series.org

Published Books – a milestone of the 50th title has been reached in September 2016!

1	Osman A. Sankoh (Mallam O.)	2001/2016	A Memoir	Hybrid Eyes – An African in Europe
2	Osman A. Sankoh (Mallam O.)	2001	Non-fiction	Beautiful Colours
3	Sheikh Umarr Kamarah	2002/2015	Poems	Singing in Exile and The Child of War
4	Abdul B. Kamara	2003/2015	A Memoir	Unknown Destination
5	Samuel Hinton	2003	Poems	The Road to Kenema
6	Karamoh Kabba	2005/2016	A Novel	Morquee – The Political Drama of Wish over Wisdom
7	Yema Lucilda Hunter	2007	A Novel	Redemption Song
8	Joe A. D. Alie	2007/2015	Research Text	Sierra Leone Since Independence – History of a Postcolonial State
9	Mohamed Combo Kamanda	2007	A Play	The Visa
10	J Sorie Conteh	2007	A Novel	In Search of Sons
11	Michael Fayia Kallon	2010/2015	A Novel	The Ghosts of Ngaingah
12	J Sorie Conteh	2011	A Novel	Family Affairs
13	Winston Forde	2011	A Play	Layila, Kakatua wan bi Lida

14	Eustace Palmer Doc P.	2012	*A Novel*	*A Pillar of the Community*
15	Siaka Kroma	2012	*Non-fiction*	*Manners Maketh Man – Adventures of a Bo School Boy*
16	Mohamed Combo Kamanda (ed)	2012	*Short Stories*	*The Price and other Short Stories from Sierra Leone*
17	Sigismond Tucker	2013	*A Memoir*	*From the Land of Diamonds to the Isle of Spice*
18	Bailah Leigh	2013	*Non-fiction*	*Dilemma of Freedom – A Diary from Behind Rebels Lines in the Sierra Leone Civil War*
19	Nnamdi Carew	2013	*A Novella*	*Tiger Fist – Two Stories*
20	Yema Lucilda Hunter	2013	*A Novel*	*Joy Came in the Morning*
21	Ebenezer 'Solo' Collier	2013	*Research Text*	<u>Primary & Secondary Education in Sierra Leone – Evaluation of more than 50 years of PRACTICES & POLICIES</u>
22	Gbananom Hallowell	2013	*Short Stories*	**Gbomgbosoro - Two Stories**
23	Sheikh Umarr Kamarah & Majorie Jones (eds)	2013	*Poems*	**beg sol noba kuk sup - An Anthology of Krio Poetry**
24	Siaka Kroma	2014	*Short*	*Tales from the Fireside*

			Stories	
25	Syl Cheney-Coker*	2014	*Poems*	*The Road to Jamaica*
26	Dr Sama Banya	2015	*A Memoir*	*Looking Back – My Life and Times*
27	Andrew K Keili	2015	*Social Commentary*	*Ponder My Thoughts – Vol. 1*
28	Jedidah A. O. Johnson	2015	*A Novel*	*Youthful Yearnings*
29	Oumar Farouk Sesay	2015	*A Novel*	*Landscape of Memories*
30	Oumar Farouk Sesay	2015	*Poems*	*The Edge of a Cry*
31	Gbanabom Hallowell	2015	*A Novel*	*The Road to Kaibara*
32	Mohamed Gibril Sesay*	2015	*A Novel*	*This Side of Nothingness*
33	Yema Lucilda Hunter	2015	*A Novel*	*Nanna*
34	Yusuf Bangura	2015	*Research Text*	*Development, Democracy & Cohesion*
35	Lansana Gberie	2015	*Research Text*	*War, Politics & Justice in West Africa*
36	Yema Lucilda Hunter	2015	*A Biography*	*An African Treasure: In Search of Gladys Casely-Hayford 1904-1950*
37	Moses Kainwo	2015	*Poems*	*Ayo Ayo Ayo and other Love Songs*
38	Abdulai Walon-Jalloh	2015	*Poems*	*Voices and Passions*
39	Gbanabom Hallowell (Ed.)	2016	*Short Stories*	*In the Belly of the Lion – An Anthology of new Sierra Leonean Short*

				Stories
40	Ahmed Koroma	2016	*Poems*	*Along the Odokoko River - Poems*
41	George Coleridge-Taylor	2016	*A Memoir*	*Transformation in Transition*
42	Karamoh Kabba	2016	*Research Text*	*Fire from Timbuktu: A Dialogue with History*
43	Umu Kultumie Tejan-Jalloh	2016	*A Memoir*	*Telling It As It Was: The Career of A Sierra Leonean Woman in Public Service*
44	Ambrose Massaquoi	2016	*Poems*	*Along the Peal of Drums: Collected Poems (1990-2015)*
45	Mohamed Gibril Sesay	2016	*Poems*	*At the Gathering of Roads (Poems)*
46	Gbanabom Hallowell	2016	*Poems*	*Manscape in the Sierra: New and Collected Poems 1991-2011*
47	Gbanabom Hallowell (Ed.)	2016	*Short Stories and Poems*	*Leoneanthology: Comtemporary Short Stories and Poems from Sierra Leone*
48	Gbanabom Hallowell	2016	*Poems*	*Don't Call Me Elvis and Other Poems*
49	Bakar Mansaray	2016	*Short Stories*	*A Suitcase Full of Dried Fish and Other Stories*
50	Gbanabom Hallowell	2016	*Poems*	*The Art of the Lonely Wanderer*

*co-published with Karantha Publishers

www.ingramcontent.com/pod-product-compliance
Lightning Source LLC
Chambersburg PA
CBHW020014050426
42450CB00005B/465